The CTO's Guide to Code Quality

PHP edition

Mark Harrison, BA, MA, MBCS

What's this book about?

This is not a book about algorithms. This is not a book about architecture. This is not a book about frameworks. This is not even a book about project management, agile or otherwise.

This is a book about "the other things" that are important to writing and maintaining a sustainable code base.

It's also a book about automation of parts of the programming process.

- If you're a CTO, the economic case for "code quality plus automation" is already strong, and getting stronger with each new iteration of hardware.
- If you're a programmer (maybe aspiring to be a CTO), it's about being able to concentrate on the stimulating, interesting, and creative parts of the craft, and getting the tedious parts done for you.

Much of the book is about the general craft of programming and helping programmers become more productive and should be useful no matter what programming language(s) you've chosen.

___

However, I find it works better to illustrate principles with examples. And the edition of the book you're currently reading picks examples from the PHP programming language.

This book will be easier to read if you are reasonably proficient in PHP... but I don't assume that, for example, you'll know what a closure is, let alone whether you'll have strong views on when to use one.

This book is divided into three main parts (after a few pages of background).

Part I is about the elements of quality code.

Part II is about individual tools to help maintain quality code.

Part III is about automation of those tools in a Continuous Integration environment.

Contents

Table of Contents

Part I: The elements of quality code

The Internet is full of pages that present false dichotomies.

A seemingly innocent questions like "should I focus on code quality, or getting things done?" contains (at least) two embedded assumptions:

- Firstly, it assumes that the things you need to do to write high-quality code lead to writing inherently more slowly than just sitting down at a keyboard and churning out code. This assumption is only true in some cases.
- Secondly, even if you were to accept the first assumption, it assumes a binary choice. It assumes that the options are writing code well or writing code quickly. This assumption is definitely false.

To see why these are assumptions, rather than absolutes, we need to think about what we mean by "high quality code."

High quality code has to do a number of things:

- It has to produce the correct outputs[1] for the "happy path"
- It has to produce the correct outputs for edge cases properly
- It needs to handle "failure elsewhere" gracefully
- It needs to be sufficiently fast (when run on its target environment)
- It has to be written in a way that takes into account its expected lifespan.

The happy path

The happy path is the route through the code where everything really worked as expected.

- In a registration form, it's the path where the new user chose a new password that met all your guidance for passwords.[2]
- Your user's login attempt gives a valid username and password.
- In a loan processing platform, it's the path where the borrower made a payment of the correct amount on the expected date.

---

[1] I'm using the term "output" fairly loosely, to mean both "output" in the purely technical sense and non-monadic side effects. Some of these footnotes are intended for more experienced practitioners.

[2] You know, like "CorrectHorseBatteryStaple"

Writing code to handle the happy path is the easy bit of the job, typically representing (for enterprise software) about 45% of the effort. Things like failure modes, logging of (and recovery from) "unexpected situations" can easily take up over half of the code base and time.

Edge cases

Edge cases are things which the simplistic happy path code won't handle, but your code needs to:

- The user picks the word "password" as their password. You probably need to catch this and give back some error asking them to pick a better password.
- The user types the wrong password. You certainly don't let them log in, and probably want to keep track of the failure.
- The borrower's payment is a few pennies short of the expected amount, or a day late, or both.

One of the most common edge cases, by the way, is that code assumes that there will be "some data" passed in, but there isn't actually any data provided at the time the code is executed. I've lost track over the years of the number of screens that are meant to show a number as a percentage of another and haven't checked for the edge case that both are zero, so you can't just divide them.

Failures

Failures are broadly when something else isn't there / isn't working, for example:

- Your code tries to update the password storage system, and you get back a database error.
- Your code tries to compare the "password"[3] that the user entered to the one you have stored, and you get back a database error.
- The database fails midway between updating the borrower's ledger and the lenders' ledger entries in a peer to peer loan that has a few hundred lenders participating in it.

Good code needs to be able to do something appropriate when it encounters either an edge case or a failure.

Sufficiently fast

"Sufficiently fast" is always an arms race. On the one hand, we have Moore's Law (and its generalisations to everything from memory to network performance.) On the other hand, we have an increase in the size of data on which we need to report and a dramatic change in user expectations.

---

[3] hashed, salted, encrypted. You aren't storing unencrypted / weakly encrypted passwords anywhere, are you?

The user expectations aren't just about the speed at which reports can be run, but the speed at which new reports / functionality can be delivered.

For many, many classes of problems, there isn't the same need to optimise for code performance that there was 20 years ago.

For many CTOs, the balance has changed dramatically - we see our hosting / service costs shrinking (for stable platforms), but our development costs increasing year on year.

The management focus has moved away from the need for application speed to development speed.

And development speed comes with focussing, not on optimisation for fast processing by CPUs, but by optimising for fast understanding of the existing code base by programmers.

Expected lifespan

Quality, to paraphrase the old ISO9001 manuals, means "fitness for purpose."

This is the point at which the previous four sections can be rewritten.

Because not all code has to cope with edge cases, failures, be easy to understand next time, or even run in less than an hour.

Sometimes, the requirement is for something ad hoc. And that means that sometimes the best solution isn't a report builder, it's just the results of a custom SQL query, run once at a console, and copy/pasted into a spreadsheet.[4]

The decision to up the quality comes when the user in question says "that was useful - I'd like that every day."

At that point, the cost economics come down on the side of "easy to maintain" over the medium term. That's the point at which you should start enforcing standards.

Security

Security was, 30 years ago, seen as an optional extra. This is no longer the case. While many of the decisions about security are primarily architectural, Quality Code needs to ensure that no vulnerabilities are inadvertently added to attack surfaces.

Writing secure code is (mostly) outside the scope of this book. However, given that many security holes are the result of local coding bugs, ensuring that code for both happy and non-happy paths are tested is part of the solution.

---

[4] Though, if you do, make sure you save the SQL. You should always have a document or a folder called something like "useful SQL queries."

Logging

Logging is sometimes seen as no more than a tool used for data recovery. Logging and backups, however, are different tools for different business purposes.

No automated tool can check whether the logging done is at an appropriate level, let alone whether data retention policies are appropriate.

However, in "GDPR is with us if we want to do business in Europe" world[5], there needs to be a mechanism both to write and purge logs. After all, data about a subject in a log is still data about a subject (and thus within the scope of Subject Access Requests.)

---

[5] Not a successful theme park, I fear.

Chapter 1: Coding style

The first decision to be made by a CTO thinking about coding style and standards is whether to bother with them.

- The argument against is that programmers are individualistic, free-thinking types who hate being constrained.
- The argument for is that programmers are co-operative types, who enjoy the praise and respect of their peers.

Both of these positions are, of course, over-simplified, and true. However, there's a key difference between the sort of programming that needs a single programmer, and the sort of programming that requires a CTO…

… and that's that we (as CTOs) have a professional duty to ensure that we minimise risks. One of those risks is the risk of over-reliance on a single individual. And part of reducing that risk is ensuring that the coding standards are sufficiently common that any programmer new to a particular block of code finds it somehow familiar. (Or, more accurately, is able to concentrate on the semantics of the code, rather than unusual syntax.)

Naming things

Coding style is about readability.

Over the short term, writing code is about instructing computers. Over the medium-to-long term, it's about communicating with the other minds that will be looking after the code.

Writing a few lines of code is cheap. Maintaining that code over years (or decades) is often several orders of magnitude too expensive. While some of the decisions are architectural[6], others are about coding style.

The worst offenders, but easiest for a code reviewer to spot, are the use of abbreviations. While a function called "getStats" (rather than getStatistics) is probably acceptable, something like "getInvalidRecoveryAttempts" is certainly clear in a way that "getIRAs" isn't.

Documenting as you go

There are many types of documentation, because there are many types of target audience. The documentation intended for a Head of Compliance in a financial company is very different from that intended for a prospective customer, let alone that of a front-line support person.

---

[6] I've heard of a function that was over 100 lines of Java to do what could (and should) have been a single left join in SQL.

While much documentation is outside of the scope of the CTO's responsibility, the question of "documentation for future programmers" most certainly is.

The best documentation is that which is immediately visible at the time you are looking at the thing being documented.

It's worth distinguishing between comments that talk about:

- what a piece of code is meant to do
- how it does it (and in some cases, why.)

Because there are tools[7] that generate documentation from DocBlocks, I recommend that DocBlock-style comments are used only for those comments you want to see in external documentation. That is to say, documentation for things like what a class represents, or what a method is intended to do.

DocBlocks start with a /** and end with a */. You can have a single line DocComment, but the more common version has multiple lines, with the first line just being the /** and the last line being the */. In this case, the intervening lines start with *.

If you are reviewing legacy code, then it's worth adding a DocBlock to a function that doesn't have one (once you understand it.) For example, is a (badly-named) function called "inc2" intended to increment the value by two, or is it version two of the increment function?

For comments that are about the "how", an inline comment (starting with //) is preferred.

A good comment should explain both what's being done, and why that approach has been chosen.

---

[7] Beyond the scope of this book

For example, a comment in the PHP that sets up a particular statement in SQL might read:

```
// This needs to include all users that
// were activated including those
// subsequently deactivated so we check
// user.activationdata IS NOT NULL
// and do NOT rely on user.status
```

Style

> The most important thing to do with coding style standards is pick one.

Like many things in IT (and technology more generally), though, there are multiple standards, and it's impossible to follow all of them, since they contradict each other.

The leading standards in the PHP coding style world are:

- PSR
- CakePHP
- Symfony
- Wordpress

There are others, such as Zend, or Fuel, that you may encounter particularly if you are inheriting a code-base.

> The best standard to pick is the one that every single member of your team agrees is the best one.
>
> *This never happens for team sizes > 3*

PSR

PSR (PHP Standards Recommendation) is a family of standards agreed upon by a group called the PHP Framework Interop Group[8]

The group includes representation from most (but not all) of the major PHP groups (particularly the framework maintainers), so code written to the PSR standards tends to "look right" to an awful lot of PHP developers.

Some of these standards are esoteric and whimsical[9], but a few are incredibly useful.

PSR1 and 2 - pure coding standards

PSR1 is described as the "basic coding standard."

It's incredibly simple, and basically mandates seven things (except that one of those things is "follow another standard.")

---

[8] Normally shortened to PHP-FIG. The PHP world love acronyms.

[9] PSR-8, the standard by which Objects written by different developers can show mutual appreciation by hugging each other. Geek humour at its finest.

1: You can open a block of PHP code with either "<?php" or "<?=", nothing else.

While different versions of the PHP language have allowed other character sets, you should avoid them.

2: You should encode all PHP files as UTF-8 without a byte-order marker.

UTF-8 is a standard for encoding characters (not just things like A, B, C, 1, 2, 3 but also *, $, ^, through to things like € and ₽.[10]

UTF-8 is a way of unambiguously encoding them. All the major browsers have supported this for over a decade.

3: Files should either define things, or actually do stuff… but not both.

PHP contains both functions and objects. Basically a file should either contain the definition of such a thing, or it should run some code there and then. So if you are including a file, you know whether you're doing stuff or simply defining stuff.

4: Class names MUST be declared in StudlyCaps.

5: Class constants MUST be declared in UPPER_CASE_WITH_UNDERSCORE_SEPARATORS.

6: Method names MUST be declared in camelCase.

---

[10] The Euro symbol and Constantine's cross, deliberately chosen to demonstrate that even the European languages contain many more symbols than just the 26 Roman letters. Thus breaking the myth that ASCII is enough for North America and Europe.

I've lumped these three together, because they are basically a way of allowing a programmer to see what kind of thing is being referenced, just by looking at how it is capitalised.

- THIS_THING must be a constant, because it's all in upper case.
- ThisThing must be an object type, because it's in StudlyCaps [Capitals at the start of each word, including the first.]
- thisThing is a method, because it's in camelCase [Capitals at the start of each word except the first.]

7: Every class must be defined in its own file, and in a namespace that includes a vendor name. It must also support the other requirements of one of the PSR autoloading standards.

PSR2 builds on top of PSR1 and defines a lot more in terms of "coding style."

The first requirement of PSR2 is that you have to follow all the requirements of PSR1.

Beyond that, it specifies things like using spaces rather than tabs for indenting, a maximum (and recommended) line length, and where spaces and new lines must, and must not go.

It's worth flagging up at this point, that many editors / IDEs have a PSR2 mode, and will automatically try to meet some of the PSR2 requirements no matter what the programmer typed.

PSR0 and PSR4 are standards to specify autoloading of classes.

PSR0 is an old standard. It's to all intents and purposes been replaced by PSR4.[11]

PSR4 is a very short standard, and basically says that classes have names that come in three parts:

1. The "vendor namespace" (which says who wrote the class),
2. Optionally, one or more subnamespaces,
3. The class name.

CakePHP

CakePHP is a PHP framework that's been around since 2005.

Many of the standards used by the Cake programmer made their way into PSR2.

---

[11] PSR3 is a standard for a logger interface.

But there are a few standards in CakePHP that weren't agreed by the rest of the PHP-FIG.

- Cake has shorter maximum line lengths.
- Cake doesn't allow ternary operators to be nested.
- Cake mandates strict rather than loose comparisons (see below.)
- Cake needs the check target of a comparison on the right[12].

The strictness of comparisons is about types.

- $a == $b evaluates as true, if $a and $b appear equal after PHP has had a go at juggling their types around.
- $a === $b evaluates as true, only if $a and $b are equal and are variables defined as the same type.

So, for example, PHP will sort of regard the value "1" as "true" in if statements, but because they are of different types

- "1 == true" evaluates as true, because PHP will treat 1 as true.
- "1 === true" evaluates as false, because 1 is an integer and true is a boolean.

---

[12] This is explained later. Explained later this is.

Symfony

Symfony, like CakePHP, is a PHP framework, and also dates from 2005.

Like CakePHP, the Symfony developers were part of the PHP-FIG, so everything in PSR2 is also part of Symfony.

Like CakePHP, the Symfony team also have some extra requirements. It's the detail of these requirements that differs.

Some of the core ones are:

- Symfony requires all the arguments of a method to be on the same line as the method name, even if that means the line is really long.
- Symfony needs the check target of a comparison on the left (see below, in the bit about Yoda.)
- Symfony likes the last item in an array to have a comma after it.
- Symfony has some specific requirements about the order of declarations in a class file.

The reason for commas in the last item in an array, by the way, is so that version comparison tools only flag up the extra lines in arrays.

Previous version of code:

```
$myarray = [
        1,
        2,
        3,
];
```

New version of code:

```
$myarray = [
        1,
        2,
        3,
        4,
];
```

Because we had a comma after the 3, even in the previous version, the only line flagged up as having changed is the line that contains the 4. If we'd not had the trailing comma, the line containing the 3 would also be flagged up as having changed.

Yoda notation (or why Symfony and Cake can't co-exist)

Yoda was, (as those of us old enough to have watched "The Empire Strikes Back" in the cinemas when it first came out will confirm), famous for putting his words in an odd order.

The term "Yoda notation" has been adopted by programmers to mean an unusual order, particularly an unusual order of "sides" in if clauses.

The normal way of reading aloud a line like "if ($value ===
null)" is to say "If dollar value is null."

Symfony prefers the way Yoda might say it "If null is the
value". That is to say the expression should be written as "if
(null === $value)."

The reason many people prefer the Yoda style is that
programmers *sometimes* mistype == or === and just type a
single equals sign. This is, of course, the way that PHP assigns
values.

But the code fragment: "$value = null" doesn't *check* whether
$value is null. It *sets* $value to null.

When this is buried in an if clause, it is almost certainly the
sort of logic error that's hard to spot. Hence Symfony prefers
the "null = $value", because that's plain-out illegal, and will
give a syntax error. (So it's easier to debug.)

Cake, on the other hand, prefers a syntax that "sounds
natural" to "easier to debug."

Wordpress

Wordpress predates both CakePHP and Symfony. As well as
being a big, popular, PHP application, it also defined its own
set of coding standards.

Unlike CakePHP and Symfony, though, Wordpress didn't
participate in the PHP-FIG, so some of its standards are
radically different.

Unless you're actually developing things like Wordpress plugins, this is probably not the right standard to choose.

The others

There are other standards around. Most of them, like Zend, PEAR[13] or Fuel, have only really caught on in one particular framework. If you are using that framework, they are a sensible choice. Otherwise…

Pick a (style) standard…

Unless you have a really specific requirement (like using Fuel or Wordpress), then PSR2 is a sensible minimum.

Both CakePHP and Symfony have their strengths and are best viewed as extensions to PSR2.

If you use either of those frameworks as a key part of your architecture, then it would be sensible to stick with the preferred standard for your framework.

Otherwise, PSR2 is a sensible compromise, allowing you to mix the Yoda syntax of Symfony with the shorter line lengths of CakePHP. (Or whatever other combination appeals.)

---

[13] You could argue that PEAR did catch on more widely, but its use fell away after the FIG published PSR-1.

Chapter 2: Testing

There are various ways to dice up the different types of testing, but one useful approach is to consider the "levels" of testing.[14]

1. Unit tests
2. Integration tests
3. System tests
4. Acceptance tests

Behaviour Driven Development (a superset of Test Driven Development that goes into more detail in the discovery process) isn't an afterthought to be considered once the code is nearing completion. It's a methodology that involves thinking hard about, and documenting (in code!) what the expected outcomes are for a bunch of different scenarios. The Happy Path typically represents about half of these scenarios, with the others being written to ensure that the code throws (and catches) appropriate errors.

---

[14] Don't mistake the levels for the "order in which you should run the tests."

Unit tests

Unit tests are simple, with all the upsides and downsides that simplicity implies.

In a unit test, one looks at a single piece of code (in PHP, either a function or an object[15]), and defines a set of tests.

Each test includes some inputs (source data) and some desired outputs. The running of the test includes giving the pre-defined inputs and checking that the outputs are as expected.

It's worth emphasising that, from a purist perspective, a unit test is very much "single piece of code." If the test involves, say, connecting to a database and relying on a set of pre-canned data stored in that database, then many people would describe it as an integration test. That having been said, the tools used to write and run unit tests can be used in a CI environment (see Part III) together with pre-prepared data that's a lot more complex than one would want to hardcode into a mock test object.

The biggest single advantage of unit tests is that they are easy to automate. (More on how to do that in PHP is in Part III of the book.)

The big disadvantage of unit tests is that they can give a false sense of security. Part of the reason for this is that simply writing a lot[16] of tests is not the same as covering all the possible cases.

---

[15] Or sometimes, just a single method of an object.

[16] An indeterminate number often defined as "the number I reached when I got bored."

Software complexity is a combinatorial problem - see the later section on Code Complexity.) The art of developing with unit tests in mind is to break code down into sections small enough to unit test comprehensively, but not so small that they are trivial. In Object-Oriented PHP, this tends to mean unit testing public methods, but not private ones. In functional[17] PHP, this is straightforward.

To give an example, consider the following code. On paper, it looks trivial, but as we dig into its testable properties, we find some issues:

```php
<?php

function pling($x) {
    if ($x===1) {
        return $x;
    }
    else {
        $y = $x * pling($x-1);
        return $y;
    }
}
```

This defines a function called pling that, on first read, appears to return the factorial of a positive integer.

---

[17] By which I mean, PHP constructed with stateless pure functions. That's to say, functions where the outputs are entirely dependent on the inputs to the function, and not on any global / external state, and where there are no side-effects. PHP provides a certain ability to do this, in a way that can be very powerful, but also very frustrating to those of us who actually want to treat PHP as if it were Haskell.

It's an incredibly nasty bit of code in some respects. On my instance of PHP:

- If you give it an input in the range 1-20, it returns an integer.
- If you give it an input in the range 21-170, it returns a double.
- If you give it an input in the range 171 to somewhere between 800,000 and 900,000, it returns the INF (the double form of infinity.)
- At some point between 800,000 and 900,000 it starts throwing (fatal) out of memory errors. The exact point varies between runs on my server.
- If you give it an input of 0, or a non-integer, it gives a fatal error.

This is unlikely to be acceptable behaviour, since having the same function return different numerical types based on the size of the input is likely to cause significant problems in any code that uses the functions.

However, in the unlikely event that it was what was needed, then we can write a suite of unit tests as follows:

- Check that pling(6) returns 720.
- Check that pling(6) returns an integer.
- Check that pling(17) returns 355687428096000.
- Check that pling(17) returns an integer.
- Check that pling(20) returns an integer.
- Check that pling(21) returns a double.
- Check that pling(100) returns a double.

To make the test code actually useful, we'd also need to write some tests such as:

- Check that pling(-1) throws an exception.
- Check that pling(1.5732) throws an exception.

As written, the code would fail these tests. This is a good thing, since it's meant that the tests have highlighted the places in which the code needs to be improved.

Checking for fatal errors automatically is something that's hard (but not impossible) to automate. It's often better to just document the bounds on which the function will fail, and make it the responsibility of the calling code to test for failure.

Writing unit tests for new code

When you are writing a new unit of code, it can be helpful to approach it in the following order:

1. Write the test(s).
2. Write some code you expect to fail the test(s).
3. Demonstrate the test fails with your dummy code.
4. Write the code you hope will pass.
5. Demonstrate the test passes with your new code (repeating steps 4 and 5 as needed.)

While programmers tend to understand the term "test driven development" (TDD) to mean following these steps, inexperienced managers sometimes think TDD just means "write unit tests and show they pass."

Writing unit tests for existing code

One of the key purposes of unit tests is to allow refactoring.

Most tutorials on Unit tests focus on the "meeting the specification in the initial version of the code." While there's no non-anecdotal data on this, my experience is that unit tests are just as useful for code that "already works."

That's because when we make a change in the way a program works, we generally want to think in terms of two things:

- The circumstances in which the new code will return the same results as the old code.
- The circumstances in which the new code will return different results from the old code.

It may be that the changes in the code are about fixing some other maintenance or performance issue, and the new code is always intended to return the same results as the old.

Unit testing can really speed up the development of new modules provided that the tests are sufficiently comprehensive.

Integration tests

Integration tests are the "next level up." They test that the units (modules) work together as expected.

A key difference is that unit testing is (normally) the job of the programmer writing / changing the piece of code in question, integration testing is normally the responsibility of someone else - a test manager, a team leader, another programmer, and while the causes of a problem can be "coding error", they are often "poor specification."[18]

It's worth noting that a powerful technique for integration testing can be to use unit testing tools with dummy data sources. However, integration testing tools are typically much more complex (and therefore take much longer to run) than unit tests.

When a test suite takes less than a minute to run, you can consider automating things so that they run literally every time a programmer saves their work.[19]

In any case, though, integration testing is firmly the domain of a development environment.

---

[18] Normally, in the sense of "only considered the happy path."

[19] Or, at least, every time they commit their code into a git repo. Most git providers have a mechanism for automating this. It's a decision for you whether this is part of the Code Review, or whether code review is something that only happens to code that can be shown to have already passed all the automated tests.

System tests

System tests are more than just big integration testing. While an integration test might consider the interactions between modules A and B, a system test, by its very nature, has to consider everything.

So, while integration tests can happily run on separate infrastructure, a system test has to consider the current state of the live environment...

... and therefore, a staging environment that is "as close to live as possible" is an important thing, as is monitoring the availability / performance of your estate.

Acceptance tests

Acceptance tests are quite different from the other tests in terms of who does them...

While the Unit, Integration and System tests are (normally) the responsibility of people who report to the CTO, the Acceptance tests are where the rest of the organisation gets involved in testing.

The more regulated the industry, the more likely it is you'll find someone called a "Head of Compliance."

> If you work in a regulated industry, a good working relationship with your Head of Compliance is as important as a good relationship with your CEO.

But as well as "it works legally", the question of whether it's acceptable to the people responsible for your customer experience is vital.[20]

Different organisations have different ways of structuring product ownership. There are a huge number of job titles in the User Experience world, and they show no sign of settling down.

Because it's about the visual design, the experience, and the outputs, the "code quality" isn't really a factor. So, while it's important, it's out of scope for this book.

---

[20] Customers can be internal people as well as external. Don't assume that your marketing people will just be happy looking at Google Analytics.

Chapter 3: Magic Numbers

Most software needs defaults. It's easier to start with an example of a magic number:

Consider a simple case — a chart. There's a limit to the number of things that can appear on a chart. So, it's common to have only the top X items shown separately, (possibly with some general category like "other" on the end to wrap up the rest.)

In a case like this, it's fairly common not to actually define the value of X up front. Instead, we get the code written, and see what it looks like on-screen, before deciding what number is correct.

This generally involves playing around with the number, and presenting a few different versions of the chart to people, and seeing what "looks right."

Somewhere in the middle of the code, there's generally a loop that looks something like:

```
$index=0;
foreach ($dataset as $row) {
        if ($index == 50) {
            break;
        }
        <some code>
        $index++;
}
```

In this particular case, we've decided that 50 points "looks right."

As the code is written, 50 is a "magic number."

> A magic number is a configuration parameter typed as a number in the middle of some code.

The reason that magic numbers are generally a bad thing is that they make configuration hard to track down. So, in a few months' time, when the product owner presents the findings of a set of customer interviews and makes the case that we need to show more detail, whichever programmer has now been assigned to making the change has to work out exactly where in the code the number of points is defined.

It may only take 5 minutes, but over the length of a product lifespan, those 5 minutes add up.

What should we do instead of magic numbers?

There are two main options, depending on where you sit on the purist to pragmatic scale.

There's a school of thought (the purist school) that says that we should pull everything out into configuration parameters separate from the codebase.

There's another school of thought (the pragmatic school) that says that having values in the codebase is acceptable, provided it's obvious what they are.

But even for purists, we normally need a default in case the parameter is missing from the configuration at runtime. So, there's still a need for embedded numbers, even if we aspire to keeping as much as possible in config.[21]

Whether you are a purist only using defaults in the codebase, or a pragmatist, the answer, in PHP, is to:

- move the number out of the middle of the code,
- turn it into a sensibly named constant, and
- put it at the top of the code module in question.

---

[21] Keeping things in config is incredibly important for any parameter that is part of a specific instance configuration - such as which database to connect to (which is likely different between production, staging, and any test instance.) This practice is more acceptable in global configuration - such as how many stories to show in a blog for a particular media type.

So you end up with code like:

```
class OurChart
{
    private const DATA_POINTS = 50;
    public function RenderChart(<params>)
    {
        $index=0;
        foreach ($dataset as $row) {
            if ($index ==
                self::DATA_POINTS) {
                break;
            }
            <some code>
            $index++;
        }
    }
}
```

It's worth noting that the numbers 0 and 1 are generally regarded as special cases, and you don't need to define a constant ONE or ZERO.[22]

Programmers coming from the C programming language may be used to having true and false defined as 1 and 0 respectively. Using numbers as booleans isn't a good idea in PHP, particularly since once in a while you get a programmer who defines them the other way round.

---

[22] A common use case is "adding one to the <global thing count>" in a loop then checking whether it's > 0 at the end. You don't use a boolean if you want to display the count at the end.

Numbered options - the evil twin of magic numbers

While they aren't strictly speaking "magic numbers" (in the sense of embedded configuration), a closely related concept is that of the numbered option.

A piece of code that sets a variable to a particular number, and then does something radically different depending on what it was set to.[23]

Instead of using numbers in this situation, it's better to use a string with a literal value for each option that helps explain the intention.

---

[23] There are numerous places where we might want code to run along the lines of "If there is one thing do X, if there are several do Y." Those aren't what I'm talking about here.

Chapter 4: Embedded configuration

Embedded configuration is the kissing cousin of magic numbers.

While a magic number embeds a business parameter in the middle of code, embedded configuration embeds a configuration value.

- The URI at which a piece of code looks for an API[24].
- The URI / hostname to which a database library attempts to establish a connection.
- The URI at which a caching service can be found.
- The access credentials for any of the above.
- Etc., Etc., Etc.[25]

Quite apart from the (potential) security vulnerabilities that might be introduced, embedded configuration makes it impossible to maintain separate dev / staging / live environments that have different configs.

---

[24] You can argue that the later members of the list are all special cases of this. My point of listing them separately is to jog your memory, not provide a taxonomy.

[25] I ran a big project for the UK's largest cinema chain, during which I was encouraged to communicate in movie quotes.

One approach is to have configuration live in a separate file, and not have that file stored in the source repo. Generally, when this is done, it's normal to store a template configuration file in the repo, so future people installing the software can easily see what to configure.

The other approach, historically regarded as more fiddly, but ultimately more flexible, is to have the configuration set in the environment. Modern deployment tools make this much more straightforward to maintain compared to a few years ago. If you are going this route, make sure there's a README that is explicit about what environment variables are required to get the code to work at all.

Chapter 5: Duplicate code

In an ideal world, code would have two[26] complementary characteristics:

- every bit of code should do only one thing (aka "separation of concerns".)
- every different thing should be done by only one bit of code (aka "Don't Repeat Yourself / DRY.")

These two rules imply that you shouldn't have identical blocks of code in your codebase.

This rule, clearly, needs parameters, both in terms of the number of tokens that have to be on a line of code for it to count as a duplicate line, and in terms of the number of lines of code that need to be in a block for the block to be counted as duplicate.

This rule, clearly, needs parameters, both in terms of the number of tokens that have to be on a line of code for it to count as a duplicate line, and in terms of the number of lines of code that need to be in a block for the block to be counted as duplicate.[27]

---

[26] Two for the moment. I'm going to be introducing more later in the book.
[27] See what I did there?

A "token" is a language element that PHP considers to be a single thing. Some tokens are single characters, like { or &. Others are words like "print" or "else". Some are short combinations, like "::"[28].

So, if we set both parameters too low, (one token, one line), then a single code line like:

```
}
```

... would flag up as a duplicate across any project more complex than "hello, world."

Less trivially, block along the lines of the following can legitimately crop up a few times in the same class:

```
foreach ($dataset as $row) {
    return (renderItem ($row));
}
```

In practice, a block of about 15 lines is a pragmatic threshold for actual repeated code.

The question of "tokens per line" is thornier. Set too low, and you get non-compliant code all over the place, set too high and you miss genuine duplication. A good starting point is the default for whatever tool you use (see Part II.)

---

[28] The :: token is known as "T_PAAMAYIM_NEKUDOTAYIM", and you used to encounter it a lot if you missed the $ sign off variable names. The parser is better at spotting the problem and giving a meaningful error message these days.

The problem with code duplication is maintainability. If there are two pieces of code that are doing "the same thing", and the requirement changes, it's normally the case that the requirement changes in both places. A common problem is that, in implementing the change, the team finds the bit of code that does the job and updates it... and fails to appreciate that there's another bit of code doing the same job elsewhere in the codebase.

The better approach, obviously, is to pull out the common section(s) and put it/them into a single place. There are a number of possible ways to do this, depending on where the duplications occur, and what your architecture looks like:

1. If the duplicated sections are in the same class, then they can become a private method of that class that both the existing blocks call.
2. If the duplicated sections are in two different classes, but those classes are both children of the same parent, then it might be appropriate to make the duplicated code a protected method of the common parent.
3. If the duplicated sections are in unrelated different classes, then they need to be pulled out into a (pure) function.[29]

Some careful thought is required, though. It's not unusual to have "almost but not quite the same" code blocks, to handle different scenarios. I'll go into this in more detail in the section about code complexity.

---

[29] We tend to implement pure functions as methods on stateless objects, rather than having global functions around. But that's an architectural preference.

DRY is good but I'm pragmatic about it. For example, pulling in a large shared library to access a single common method would be overkill.

Chapter 6: Unused code

Code should be there for a reason.

Sometimes the actual reason a piece of code is still there is "we used to use this bit of code, then re-engineered elsewhere and didn't notice that we were no longer using this bit...."

The easy / lazy approach is simply to put the offending section into a comment block.

Try to resist the temptation.

Modern version control systems generally make it very easy to go back and find the deleted code if, at some point in the future, you find you did have a use for it after all.

Sometimes, however, the reason is "the unused code came with <some other thing> we added to our project."

Generally, it's not a good idea to copy/paste someone else's entire code files into your codebase. [Copying a few lines is generally OK, but it's better to actually understand your code than include someone else's lines in your own codebase.]

If you want to include an object / function / framework, then that's an architectural matter rather than a code quality matter. With frameworks, that's a big decision, and any framework is likely to contain things that you don't need. That can be fine...

However, with third party objects / libraries, there's often a better approach:

If you want to use the object / library "as is", then use a tool like Composer to manage those dependencies, and just ensure that you are bringing in the right version of the object / library.

If you want to use an object / library, but want to enforce some standards about how it's used, or do some things a different way, then it can be better to use Composer to install the third-party tool, write a wrapper object / function for it, and have the rest of your code call your wrapper.

If you want to use an object / library, but there are some bugs, then it's generally better practice to contribute back to the project and use the "fixed version." Obviously, this isn't always possible. In this case, it may be worth including your (fixed) fork of third-party tool in your code until such time as the object / library maintainers fix things.

It's this third scenario that can lead to unused code in your core codebase. There are no easy answers in this situation. However, the same principle of using a version control system rather than commenting out old code applies.

Chapter 7: Code complexity / size

Books have been written about code complexity... but there are two key ideas:

Key idea one, the more complex something is, the harder it is to understand (and understanding something is a necessary precondition to changing it successfully.)

Key idea two: there's a balance to be struck between:

- How many things there are.
- How complex each individual thing is.

I'm using the word "thing" here to refer to any / all of objects, methods, parameter lists, fields and the like.

> A good heuristic is that an "understandable" block of code is a block of code that can be viewed on-screen in one go.

As a simple example, consider a case from the finance industry. A common regulatory requirement is that lenders fall into different categories, with only "sophisticated" lenders allowed to purchase or sell certain products.[30] To make things more complex, certain products can become non-tradeable, or only tradeable with appropriate warnings.[31]

In a case like this, it may well be that the code started out with a much simpler set of requirements, but the number of cases has expanded over time. Perhaps, instead of displaying nothing when a loan isn't tradeable because the lender isn't flagged as sophisticated, Marketing now want us to show a call to action to offer than lender the chance to self-certify as sophisticated...

---

[30] Sophisticated is regulator-speak for "it's OK if Gordon Gecko loses money, we're only here to protect granny's life savings. But if we call Gordon sophisticated, he feels good about not having protection."

[31] For example, in Peer to Peer lending, it's fairly common to restrict trading between lenders to only happen with loans that are in good standing. Once the borrower starts skipping payments, trading can be suspended.

So we've ended up with code like:

```
public function
renderTextForLoanPurchase($lender, $loan) {
    $output = "";
    switch ($loan->standing) {
        case "GoodStanding":
            <code line 1.1>
            <code line 1.2>
            <code line 1.3>
            <code line 1.4>
            <code line 1.5>...
            break;
        case "NeverTradeable":
            <code line 2.1>
            <code line 2.2>
            <code line 2.3>
            <code line 2.4>
            <code line 2.5>...
            break;
        case "SophisticatedTradeable":
            if ($lender->sophistication()) {
                <code line 3.1>
                <code line 3.2>
                <code line 3.3>
                <code line 3.4>
                <code line 3.5>...
            } else {
                <code line 4.1>
                <code line 4.2>
                <code line 4.3>
                <code line 4.4>
                <code line 4.5>...
            }
            break;
    }
    return $output;
}
```

There might, of course, be rather more than 5 lines of code for each case...

In this case, the code might be better as something like:

```
public function
renderTextForLoanPurchase($lender, $loan) {
    $output = "";
    switch ($loan->standing) {
        case "GoodStanding":
            $output=$this->
                renderGoodStanding(...);
            break;
        case "NeverTradeable":
            $output=$this->
                renderNonTradeable (...);
            break;
        case "SophisticatedTradeable":
            $output=$this->
                renderSophisticated(...);
            break;
        }
    return $output;
}


private function renderGoodStanding(...) {
    ...
}

private function renderNonTradeable(...) {
    ...
}

private function renderSophisticated (...) {
    ... if clause for lender type goes here
    ...
}
```

In this case, the overall length of the code is slightly longer[32], but it's now split into four sections, each of "at a glance" complexity.

Measuring complexity

The overall complexity of our system is normally pretty much a given.[33]

However, we can control the maintainability of the codebase by breaking the overall system up into understandable sections. Sometimes this means more classes, sometimes more methods.

Some measures of complexity in PHP relate to individual methods:

- Cyclomatic complexity
- NPath complexity
- Method length (in terms of lines of code)

Others relate to the class overall:

- Class length (in terms of lines of code)
- Number of methods
- Number of public methods
- Number of fields

---

[32] Depending on your architecture, you may want pure functions (and thus pass parameters around,) or have everything in object variables. I'm passing them into the main function because it's easier for demo purposes and saves lines on class variables :-)

[33] OK, outside the scope of this book. A core CTO skill is to continue to argue for simplicity where possible.

Clearly, the first two need some more detailed explanation, but before I do that, a TANSTAAFL[34] warning:

> Some of the techniques for reducing one measure of complexity increase a different measure of complexity.

This is because there are basically two tools we can use to change complexity:

1. Splitting out the methods within an object class
2. Creating new object classes

Clearly, if we split out methods within a class, the method gets simplified, but the number of methods in the class increases. So we do need to understand (apart from the one-screen heuristic) what the Cylomatic and NPath complexities actually are.

---

[34] There ain't no such thing as a free lunch.

Cyclomatic complexity (decision points count)

Cyclomatic complexity is a measure of the number of decision points in a method.

Considering the long name, it's actually a simple measure. If it had been called "Decision Points Count", it might have been used more.

Calculating cyclomatic complexity

While there's a theoretical description based on the algebraic characteristics of the flow graph, you don't need to be a mathematician to understand how to calculate it for some PHP code.

The general rule in the PHP world[35] is that it's:

- 1,
- plus the number of if statements[36],
- plus the number of while statements,
- plus the number of cases in switch(es),
- plus the number of for statements.

---

[35] I'm foreshadowing (your clue to quality literature) Part 2 here. The use of one particular tool has basically standardised the way the PHP world calculates Cyclomatic complexity.

[36] But not elseif statements, which doesn't entirely make sense.

Consider the following section of code:

```
if ($a) {
    <do something>;
}

if ($b) {
    <do something>;
}

switch ($fruit) {
    case "apples":
        <do something>;
        break;
    case "oranges":
        <do something>;
        break;
    case "bananas":
        <do something>;
        break;
}
```

There are two if statements, and three cases, so our cyclomatic complexity is:

- 1,
- plus the number of if statements = 2,
- plus the number of while statements = 0,
- plus the number of cases in switch(es) = 3,
- plus the number of for statements = 0.

Which is to say 1 + 2 + 3 = 6.

Sensible values for cyclomatic complexity

The generally accepted rule of thumb is that:

- 1-4 is regarded as low complexity
- 5-7 is regarded as moderate
- 8-10 is regarded as high complexity
- 11+ is regarded as very high

Having lots of code with a low cyclomatic complexity may be a sign of a simple code base... but may, of course, mean that everything is being broken down too much, and you will have free lunch problems later.

High cyclomatic complexity code is probably a good candidate for refactoring the next time changes that involve it are implemented.

Very high cyclomatic complexity code should ideally be refactored (in a way that doesn't change its functionality / passes regression) before the next changes are made.

NPath complexity

Despite the simpler name, NPath complexity is more sophisticated, but is a better metric for the overall complexity of a method.

While cyclomatic complexity just measures the number of decision points, NPath counts the number of possible paths through the code.

If we consider the same code we saw above (with its two if statements, and three switch cases), we can think about the code in the following way:

- There are two possible things that might have happened in the first if, either it ran the code or it didn't.
- There are two possible things that might have happened in the second if, either it ran the code or it didn't.
- There are four possible things that might have happened in the switch. Either it ran one of the three cases, or it didn't.

But each of these is independent of the previous flow, so we have to multiply the options together to get the number of possible paths.

So, the NPath complexity of the code is 2 * 2 * 4 = 16
Uj

NPath complexity can get high quickly. A threshold of 200 is generally the point at which some refactoring might be indicated. It's not uncommon to have much, much, higher NPath numbers... we routinely see code with NPath numbers in the tens of thousands before refactoring.

Code with high NPath/cyclomatic complexity can be impossible to unit test due to the large number of paths through the code.

How many parameters?

One of the problems with complexity is that applications, overall, are complex, and sometimes we need to do things that genuinely contain lots of data.

Consider a method called addStaffMember, on a StaffMember object.

When we start development, we might have a list of mandatory fields we need to know about the user:

- Familyname (name)
- Knownas (name)
- Email address
- Extension
- Building
- Department

With six fields, it feels cleaner to have a method that looks like:

```
public function addStaff(
   $familyname,
   $knownas,
   $email,
   $extension,
   $building,
   $department
   ) { ...
   }
```

This certainly feels better code than passing in an array called $data, and then trying to decode $data["familyname"] and so on.

But as time progresses, scope creeps, and we have more fields that the combination of HR, legal, and office facilities, want. Maybe a job title comes next… and over time the number of parameters increases.[37]

And we hit a threshold of "too complex" according to whatever default we set.

This is an example of where human intelligence and coding experience is more important than inflexible "rules."

---

[37] Put aside for this purpose the question of whether this is opening the object in the sense of Open-closed (see chapter 8). What matters here is that we end up with lots of fields.

Chapter 8: SOLID code

In Chapter 5, I mentioned two principles of good code, but promised to introduce more later.[38]

SOLID principles

There is a set of code principles known as SOLID, because of an acronym used to remember them. I don't find the acronym particularly useful, because the L stands for Liskov substitution, and by the time you understand that, you are probably beyond the stage where you need little acronyms to remember short lists.

The principles are:

Single responsibility

Each part of the code should have only one reason to change. A change in the specification for that thing will require a change in that module of code... however, a change anywhere else in the specification won't require a code change in that module.

---

[38] At least, I did if you read the footnotes.

Of course, a change in the general specification might require a change in the specification for multiple modules. But, for example, a decision to change the presentation of a number on-screen should normally be separate from the calculation of that number (in anything other than the most trivial codebases.)

Open-closed

The principle is that once a module is released, it should be possible to extend it (open for extension), but not possible to change the source code (closed for modification.)

Clearly the two principles are at odds with each other. You can't change what it does without changing the source code.

In the C++ world, where the Open-closed principle was first proposed, the solution was to keep existing modules, but provide "abstraction servers" (or, as we tend to call them, wrappers.)

As such, this principle is far from universally adopted. We generally accept that it should be possible to change some code to a new version when the requirement changes. Source control systems and regression testing software has become a lot better over the last couple of decades, and a regression difference is only a test failure if it relates to a part of the specification that hasn't changed.

Liskov substitution

When you create a subtype (child class) of an object, it should be possible to replace uses of the original (parent) object with uses of the new child.

The reverse clearly isn't true. The whole point of creating a child is to create additional functionality.

In practice, to follow Liskov substitution, we shouldn't over-write methods from the parent class, but only create new methods.

The purpose of this is, obviously, regression. If we are changing code to use a new (child) class, then it's not unreasonable to expect the code to use a new method on the parent at the same time.

A classic example of something that breaks Liskov substitution is implementing a class called "square (side)" which extends an existing class called "rectangle (side 1, side 2.)" Because using a square forces the sides to be the same length, you can't generally use a square object instead of a rectangle one.

Liskov substitution is a principle to consider, but not always a principle that it's pragmatic to uphold. Given the way that PHP class extension works, it's often worth writing non-Liskov code. The key thing is how future programmers will understand it.

Interface segregation

It's generally regarded as better to have different interfaces (public methods) to different modules, rather than one big "do everything" method.

When it comes to object classes, this is generally useful.[39]

Dependency inversion

I can't help but feel that this name was created to give the acronym DIP to "Dependency Inversion Principle."[40] [41]

The idea is simple. You should always depend on the abstractions presented, rather than the actual implementation of a module / class. It's worth noting that the word "abstractions" in this context doesn't mean quite the same thing as a PHP abstract class.

Instead, it means that you should avoid public variables in class definitions, but instead use explicit methods to get and set such things (if and only if you need them.) I'll start by using a really simple example - something that uses a customer ID.

---

[39] APIs are different. Parameter validation, for example, is commonly done through a framework which presents each call in a RESTful way.

[40] It predates the SOLID acronym, so can't be that.

[41] This probably says more about me than it does about the author of the original paper, Robert C. Martin.

Some bad code would look as follows:

```
class DemoOfBadPractice {
    public $customerid = 0;
    // default customer ID

    public function getCustomerid() {
        return $this->customerid;
    }
}
------------
$customer = new DemoOfBadPractice;
$customer->customerid = 76;
echo $customer->getCustomerid();
```

One problem, in this case, is that simply allowing the calling code to set a value opens the codebase up to all kinds of injection attacks.

So, instead, we can use something like:

```
class DemoOfBetterPractice {
    private $customerid = 0;
    // default customer ID

    public function setCustomerid($newid) {
        $this->customerid = $newid;
    }

    public function getCustomerid() {
        return $this->customerid;
    }
}
------------
$customer = new DemoOfBetterPractice;
$customer->setCustomerid(76);
echo $customer->getCustomerid();
```

OK, at this point, we're still open to injection attacks, but now
we have a way to protect against them:

```
class DemoOfBestPractice {
    private $customerid = 0;
    // default customer ID

    public function setCustomerid($newid) {
        <SOME CODE TO VALIDATE THE NEW ID>
        $this->customerid = $newid;
    }

    public function getCustomerid() {
        return $this->customerid;
    }
}
------------
$customer = new DemoOfBestPractice;
$customer->setCustomerid(76);
echo $customer->getCustomerid();
```

This principle isn't just about protecting from injection. It's
also about allowing a complete substitution of a module by
something that works differently (internally.) It has another
benefit - namely that it makes testing much more
straightforward to automate.

For example, a common requirement for application
scalability is to have some kind of caching layer in front of
some form of data store. This data store is sometimes a
database, but could just as easily be a remote API call to do
something like map a postcode to LatLong cordinates, or
interface with a customer record in Salesforce.

We all understand how this codebase should be structured to allow swapping out of these backing services. We sometimes miss that the caching layer itself should be swappable.[42]

So rather than having our code use the "library du jour" to interface directly with memcached, say, we should create a service called "ourCache" and ensure that it only presented suitable methods. In particular, it shouldn't present any methods that are specific to the fact we're using memcached.

So, our "ourCache" class shouldn't present an addServer() method. There's no getting around the fact that the standard php memcached library has such a method, but the use of that method should be concentrated in one place, not every place that needs a caching layer.

A side benefit of doing this is that it, again, makes unit testing more straightforward, because we can swap in a mock caching object.

Specific PHP practices that (sometimes) arise from SOLID

There are a number of PHP practices that have arisen from programmers trying to follow SOLID principles. These tend to be more contentious among programmers, and there can be good use cases for them.

---

[42] Even if I agreed that Redis were always superior to memcached (and I don't, by the way), then I don't have a crystal ball to tell me what will ultimately replace Redis.

In general, though, we're now firmly in the territory of talking about banning techniques that more expert programmers can find very useful, but have sufficient pitfalls that more junior programmers may find problematical.

It's up to the CTO to determine whether to put in place rules to avoid these techniques completely (and thus optimise for less-skilled programmers) or allow them (and optimise for code that more experienced programmers might find more straightforward.)

Avoiding Static Access

Many people will program in PHP for years without encountering static access.

They are (sort of) global functions that can use a raw class rather than creating an object of that class.

That is to say, rather than running:

```
$myobject = new SomeClass{};
$myvariable = $myobject->someMethod($params);
```

... we can instead run ...

```
$myvariable = SomeClass::someMethod($params);
```

Viewed one way, this is just a way of creating a set of global functions (which happen to use a namespace.)

For pure functions, this would, on its own, be a good thing.

The problem with static methods / values in PHP classes is that they can have side-effects, which make testing and debugging very hard (such as changing state within static class variables.)

Avoid else clauses in objects

The if-then-else syntax has been with us for a long time. It's in Algol 60, for example, and has been used in everything from LISP to Basic.

However, some programmers, particularly those who came to higher-level languages from low level languages, grew up in a world where they were to be avoided.[43] The reasons normally cited are that they find it easier to follow code flow with fewer indents. Other programmers find explicit IF / ELSE branches easier to follow than early returns.

Another reason that many organisations enforce this rule tends to be about "use of particular tools" (see Part II), since one of the most popular PHP code quality tools has a strong viewpoint on them.

The following code is (if we accept this rule) regarded as bad:

```
if (...check...) {
    // some code to calculate $returnvalue
} else {
    // some code to calculate $returnvalue
}
return $returnvalue;
```

---

[43] The reasons are well beyond the scope of this book, but basically to do with branch prediction efficiency.

The following code is preferred (under this "rule"):

```
if (...check...) {
    // some code to calculate $returnvalue
    return $returnvalue;
}

// some code to calculate $returnvalue
// <only executed if we haven't already
returned>

return $returnvalue;
```

Avoid assignments within if clauses

Generally, when we write an if clause, we are wanting just to make a comparison. So a common thing, particularly among more junior programmers (and programmers who have to flip between PHP and another language), is to write code like:

```
if ($value = 1) {
    // some code to calculate $returnvalue
    return $returnvalue;
}
```

At first glance, this looks like it will only run when $value equals 1.

This misses the point that = is an assignment operator, not a "check for equality" operator.

So the code above assigns the value 1 to the variable $value, and then always runs the code in the if condition.

The code that was required is:

```
if ($value == 1) { // or ($value === 1)
    // some code to calculate $returnvalue
    return $returnvalue;
}
```

Because such constructions are 99% likely to be typos, it's easier just to ban them, and implement automated testing for them.[44]

Duplicate array keys

There's a common technique in programming that:

1. Assigns a default value to a variable.
2. Runs some code that, under some circumstances assigns a specific value to the variable.

Doing this with simple variables isn't a problem.

However, defining an array where the same array key is repeated several times, and relying on the code that picks up the array to work out which value is needed is fraught with problems.

---

[44] See also the previous chapter on magic numbers

So the following is fine, because it builds the array, then returns the final version, which contains only one "dummy" row:

```
$returnarray = [];
$returnarray['dummy']="default";
$returnarray['dummy']="newvalue";
return $returnarray;
```

But the following isn't:

```
return [
    'dummy' => "default",
    'dummy' => "newvalue",
    ]
```

Boolean arguments that change what a function calculates

If a method includes code that processes a boolean argument, and then decides what to do depending on which argument it gets, it's generally a sign that the class is in danger of getting too complex.

In this case, it may be better to consider one of:

- A new method to handle the case where "condition = false", and calling that method instead of the original one when the condition is false.
- Two new methods, one for true and one for false, and having the calling code work out which one to call.

It's worth noting that a variant of this is when there's a boolean parameter in a class constructor function... in this case, building a new class is often a better way to go.[45]

---

[45] Generally, but not always, this new class can be a child of the original.

Chapter 9: "Database" interaction

Which "database" are we discussing?

I'm also going to use the term "database" fairly broadly and include the likes of key-value stores (like memcached.)

This is not a book about architecture. The question of when SQL databases and NoSQL databases are a better fit for an application is well outside of its scope.

Likewise, the question of whether to use a database-specific library (like MySQLi) or a database-agnostic library (like PDO) is more nuanced than a belief that "changing database servers" is either something likely to happen, or something that would somehow be straightforward if only you had used the right library all along.

I'm also going to side-step the question of whether you should create database connections and pass them into objects or have object code create its own connections. This is, again, because this is an architectural matter and well outside the scope of this book.

If you are coding against a framework that abstracts all the database calls off behind a DAO access, you can safely skip this chapter... however, while the DAO is a useful design pattern, there are other cases where writing SQL statements leads to better overall application maintainability and performance.

Connections, configuration, and prefixes

If there is one thing worse than a magic number, it's an embedded set of connection credentials.

If you aren't using a framework that already does this for you, then starting with an object class that is either a wrapper or an extension of your chosen library that does the following is worthwhile:

- Queries your configuration (whether that lives in a file or the environment) and determines:
    a. The address of database server[46],
    b. The access credentials,
    c. The "prefix / database", which is to say, either the database name, or the caching prefix (in a key-value store).
- Opens your connection.

For "complex databases", like SQL, this object is normally an extension, so you can then use the library's normal methods in the rest of your code.

---

[46] I'm just going to use the word "server" to mean server / cluster throughout.

For "simple databases" like key-value stores, this object is normally a wrapper, so you can add a key prefix to anything you store, which has two advantages:

- Even if your dev, staging, and live instances end up sharing the same infrastructure[47], there is no risk of multiple environments overwriting each others' values in cache.
- You can have multiple staging environments[48].

Table naming conventions (in SQL)

There is less consistency of standards in naming tables than in the PHP world. It's another area where "having a standard and sticking to it" tends to be better than not doing so.

We prefer that table names should be in the plural, and rows in the singular, so a query looks like:

```
SELECT employee FROM employees WHERE ...
```

Other naming conventions prefer collective nouns for table names:

```
SELECT employee FROM staff WHERE ...
```

---

[47] This is common with services like Amazon Elasticache.

[48] This is a regular requirement in some industries, particularly those with strict compliance regimes, and helps non-IT people analyse new versions of the code on particular data sets.

Case sensitivity in SQL statements

MySQL, the most popular database, publishes coding standards[49] that recommends that:

- Tables should be named in lowercase.
- Columns should be named in lowercase.
- Keywords should be written in UPPERCASE.

Indenting in SQL statements in source code

As ever, it is better to have a standard than not.

The more complex the SQL, the more likely it is that two separate issues will arise:

1. Individual queries will take a long time to run.
2. The programmer asked to maintain the (PHP) code will have a different level of SQL skills to the programmer who originally wrote the SQL.

The question of whether SQL should remain fully normalised, or allow aggregation (for things like management reports, possibly on a batch basis) is straying firmly into the scope of architecture, so beyond this book.

---

[49] https://dev.mysql.com/doc/internals/en/coding-style.html Strictly, these are coding standards for writing tests, but the general principles are sound.

We prefer that the following keywords should start new lines (in source code):

- SELECT
- UPDATE
- INSERT
- [INNER / OUTER / LEFT / RIGHT] JOIN ... but the ON clause continues the same line
- SET
- FROM
- WHERE
- AND (in a where clause, optional new line in a JOIN ON clause)
- GROUP BY (but see below)
- ORDER BY (but see below)

If there are multiple fields in a GROUP BY / ORDER BY clause, then we allow them to be on the same line if the line length remains within the guideline for the coding standard we're using.

Using prepared statements

Prepared statements have been available in the major libraries for some years. Even if you are cleansing the data in some other way[50], having a defence-in-depth approach to hacking is a sensible approach.

Prepared statements are not only a way around this, but (sometimes) have some performance advantages.

They are a technique that enforces a separation of the logic of the query from the values being passed to the database. While there's a small learning curve if you've not encountered them before, once you understand that, this separation makes them easier to understand (for complex queries) once you do.

The performance advantages come when you are running a loop with the same query (with different values) many (N) times. In this case, there are N+1 round trips to the database server - one to set up the query, and N to pass in the values. For higher values of N, this "one extra trip" is outweighed by the fact that the server only needs to parse the structure of SQL once, and each subsequent set of values is queried faster.

The break point as to how big N needs to be both changes over time as database versions come and go, and depends on the complexity of your query, so it's fair to say that the biggest benefit is security.

---

[50] It's worth noting, by the way, that using the PHP standard "real_escape_string" doesn't remove percent signs and underscores.

It's worth noting that a prepared statement flow takes more lines of code than a "mashed" statement. However, given that we're optimising for security, then legibility, once programmers are familiar with them, the number of lines shouldn't be the tail that wags the dog.

To demonstrate this, we assume that the variable $surname is a string, and that the variable $mysqli is a database connection:

Non-prepared statement version of code:

```
$sql = SELECT employee
    FROM employees
    WHERE employee_surname = "$surname";
$result=$mysqli->query($sql);
```

Prepared statement version of code (in the MySQLi syntax - the PDO syntax is a bit different):

```
$sql = SELECT employee
    FROM employees
    WHERE employee_surname = "?";
$stmt = $mysqli->prepare ($mysql);
$stmt->bind_param('s', $surname);
$stmt->execute();
$result = $stmt->fetch();
```

The problem that we're fixing, is of course, the situation where the variable $surname has been set, through some poorly parsed user-generated input, to a value like "Billy); DROP TABLE customers;"[51]

---

[51] What, you were expecting him to be called "Bobby"?

PART II: Tools

This part of the book does not pretend to be an exhaustive list of the tools that are available. Instead, it focuses on the (publicly available) tools that the author actually uses.

Neither is it intended to be a comprehensive guide to using the tools included.

In particular, there will be no mention of how to install the tools in question for two reasons:

- How you'd install the tools for use by a single programmer on their own computer is often very different from how you'd install them for use in a CI system.
- The tools tend to be updated regularly.

There is a logic to the order they're presented in, however. That's the order in which I[52] run them.

This order, in turn, is based around ensuring that the "most urgent" checks are run first. That's to say, if a piece of code is going to fail unit testing, and therefore needs to be changed, it doesn't matter so much whether it would pass PSR-2 compliance.

---

[52] Or more precisely, my CI system

> As a CTO, you have to set your requirements.
> Particularly when the project involves taking on an
> existing code base.
>
> The perfect is the enemy of the good.

It may be entirely acceptable to you to go live with code that's been refactored (while still passing unit testing), to reduce complexity, even if the refactoring doesn't reduce the NPath complexity down to your target.

It is nice to get daily reports of violation counts so you can manage this part of the technical debt problem, ensuring that things improve over time.

Chapter 10: PHPUnit for unit testing

PHPUnit is the de facto standard, currently on release 8 (having first been released back in 2004.)

PHPUnit provides:

- A PHP class called PHPUnit\Framework\TestCase.
- A command-line tool to run tests written by the programmer.
- Lots of other things like mock object generation.

Writing a PHPUnit test

At the simplest level, a test (for a class) looks like the code block coming soon. (This is live code from a client.)

In this case, it's assumed that we have written a class called Render in the namespace OurOrg\Frontend.

The class has a method called getFormattedDate which takes a string containing a date, and a timezone, and returns them in a particular format.

The reason we've written our own class is twofold:

- Firstly, we wanted to standardise the way that dates are shown throughout the site, so if that ever changes, we can change the render function in one place, rather than looking for every time we print a date.
- Secondly, while the tests included in this book don't show it, our class also shows the words "today", "yesterday" and "tomorrow" instead of the actual date where appropriate, so we couldn't use a simple DateTime->format command anyway.

So, we write a test file called RenderTest.php which contains the following:

```php
<?php

namespace OurOrg\Frontend;

use PHPUnit\Framework\TestCase;

class RenderTest extends TestCase
{
    private $render;
    protected function setUp(): void
    {
        $this->render=new Render;
    }

    public function testEpochStart()
    {
        $result = $this->render->
            getFormattedDate("1970-01-23",
            "GMT");
        $this->assertEquals(
            "Fri 23 Jan 1970", $result);
    }

    public function testMarksBirthday()
    {
        $result = $this->render->
            getFormattedDate("1970-10-20",
            "GMT+1");
        $this->assertEquals(
            "Tue 20 Oct 1970", $result);
    }
}
```

Let's take the code a step at a time:

```php
<?php
namespace OurOrg\Frontend;
use PHPUnit\Framework\TestCase;
```

We're writing a PHP file that uses an object in our standard namespace but extends the PHPUnit-provided class "Framework\TestCase."

```php
class RenderTest extends TestCase
```

We create a new object class, named after the Object we want to test, with the word "Test" added.) This class extends the TestCase method provided by PHPUnit, which means we can inherit a bunch of protected methods.

```php
private $render;
```

We're going to create an object called $render, from which various of the tests will be calling methods later. We set this up as a private variable.

```php
protected function setUp(): void
{
    $this->render=new Render;
}
```

We run the special function setUp. This is a function that the PHPUnit command tools will look for and run at the start of each test run. From this point onwards, our test code can call methods on $this->render.

```
public function testEpochStart()
{
    $returnedDate = $this->render->
        getFormattedDate("1970-01-23",
        "GMT");
    $this->assertEquals(
        "Fri 23 Jan 1970", $returnedDate);
}
```

PHPUnit's runtime is going to be looking for public methods in our class and running them.

This method is used to test the formatting of a date. So we create a local variable called $returnedDate, and get the return of the getFormattedDate method on our Render class with some appropriate (hard-wired) test data.

The assertEquals method checks that the "hardwired" string we provided matches the result the function under test generated. As well as asserting that results are equal, PHPUnit has many other types of assertion which are useful, particularly for things off the happy path.

Unit testing datetime has interesting problems. You can sometimes generate non-deterministic tests which fail say 1% of the time. While you might never encounter this in the testing run by individual programmers, in a CI system, a 1% false positive rate can be very time-consuming. A common problem is when the clock has ticked over to give a different time between the code and the test working out what "now" is.

Other types of test

Checking for a specific value isn't the only type of test assertion that PHPUnit can check for.

The total list of assertions is long, but the most useful include:

- Whether a return is null.
- Whether a return is true.
- The type of a return (with many specific tests for individual types as well as a "check class" assertion.)
- Various numerical comparisons (>, >=, <, <=.)
- Whether a (string) return matches a format or a regular expression.
- Whether files/directories exist, and their attributes (which makes PHPUnit useful in the realm of system testing, not just pure unit testing.)
- Whether an object returned from a factory is an instance of a particular class or interface.

The "equals" tests come in various flavours, to enable XML and JSON objects to be checked for, as well as things like case sensitivity.

Data Providers in PHPUnit

While simple unit tests include the "expected value" in the body of the test code, PHPUnit contains a standard mechanism for providing a set of tests.

So instead of writing a set of tests of the form:

```
$result = $this->render->
    getFormattedDate("1970-01-23",
        "GMT");
$this->assertEquals(
    "Fri 23 Jan 1970", $result)

$result = $this->render->
    getFormattedDate("1970-01-24",
        "GMT");
$this->assertEquals(
    "Sat 24 Jan 1970", $result)
```

We can use a "data provider" to separate out the test data from the "test code execution." PHPUnit inspects the docblock (ie - PHP comment) just before the function to see whether they contain a directive that the function should use a different function as its data source.

In this case, we'd write code as follows[53]:

```php
/**
 * @dataProvider myDataSource
 */
public function testDateRender($input,
    $inputTZ, $expected)
{
    $result = $this->render
    ->getFormattedDate($input, $inputTZ);
    $this->assertEquals($expected,
    $result);
}

public function myDataSource()
{
    return [
        ["1970-01-23", "GMT", "00:00 Fri
23 Jan 1970"],
        ["1970-01-24", "GMT", "00:00 Sat
24 Jan 1970"],
        ["2019-07-22", "GMT", "00:00 Mon
22 Jul 2018"],
    ]
}
```

It's worth noting that, in most cases, the array of values will contain a set of arrays, where each of those subarrays contains:

- The parameters we're going to pass the function we're ultimately trying to test
- The expected result from that test

---

[53] Different versions of PHPUnit have had different "views" on whether the prefix "test" is what's needed here. The examples given use the prefixes preferred by the official documentation for version 8.3, the latest at time of writing.

Running PHPUnit will (assuming the object we're trying to test is correct) show the count of tests/assertions it made, and the details of any that failed.

Backfitting PHPUnit to legacy code

As we said in Part I, sometimes we're not using PHPUnit to test brand new code, but to regression test existing code (as a precursor to making changes to it.)

In this case, a common pattern is to:

1. write a set of unit tests, which include obviously bogus "expected" values
2. run those, watch them fail
3. copy/paste the "actual value" from the PHPUnit console output into the "expected" value in code

Clearly, this is a lot more straightforward in simple data types (strings, numbers and the like) than it is with methods that return objects.

But when the objects are returning primitive types, and you are happy that the code is actually already working in all cases (including those off the happy path) then this can be a very quick way to build a regression test suite.

Working with mock objects

Many objects that take other objects as their parameters (either in their constructor or as parameters to individual methods.)

When unit testing it's often useful to have a "placeholder" that looks like one of these "objects passed in". A mock object is one that presents the same methods as a live object, but does not rely on the internals of that object.

PHPUnit allows creation of a mock object in a single line of code. These single-line mock objects automatically present all the methods that their class would, but always return null. (Additional lines of code are, of course, needed to simulate non-null returns.)

In the following example we have two classes:

- One called RenderWording, which has methods to return various English words depending on the type of customer (for example, the word "pupil" when the customer is of type "school", or "person" when the customer is of type "company.")
- One called RenderOverviewTable which has a method to return a block of HTML based on being given things like a name.

In this particular case, the architect has put the RenderWording object into the constructor parameters on the RenderOverviewTable, and the other data into the specific method parameters.

To build unit tests for the RenderOveviewTable class (which are, of course, separate from the unit tests for the RenderWording class) we create a mock RenderWording object, and pass that into the RenderOverviewTable as follows:

```
class RenderOverviewTableTest extends TestCase
{
    private $overviewtable;
    protected function setUp(): void
    {
        $stub = $this->
            createMock(RenderWording::class);
        $this->overviewtable = new
            RenderOverviewTable($stub);
    }
...tests go here...
]
```

At that point, we can test the individual methods by passing in the dummy data required to test things on the happy and other paths.

Mocks vs Dummy data

For non-trivial code, specifically code where objects take objects as parameters (rather than primitive data types), there are two main approaches for testing.

One approach is to use mock objects which, as we've seen, PHPUnit makes easy.

The other approach is to use the live codebase and pass in real objects, but use a dummy set of underlying data. With this approach, the tests are written to check for the expected return of objects that are (ultimately) processing the dummy data.

Before the growth of CI systems (see part III), it was common practice to make mocks for everything.
Increasingly, though, it's becoming common to have a CI system spin up a "dummy instance", prepopulated with a dummy database.[54] The key advantage of this approach is that it removes the "incorrect code in the mock" problem as a potential source of errors.

Which approach is preferable depends on the extent to which your CI system can automate such dummy data. And this pretty much comes down to ensuring you have no configuration living within the source code.

Even in architectures that depend on third-party services, the mainstream services commonly provide sandbox systems, or allow dummy accounts for testing. The providers of these sandboxes were probably imagining humans running trial code by hand. Unless there are throughput limits on the number of calls that can be made to a sandbox, there's no reason to restrict your testing approach to having to use mocks.

That having been said, mocks can be much faster (because you avoid the overhead of spinning up or connecting to these services), so have a place.

---

[54] Prior to GDPR, it was relatively common to have this "dummy data" be a snapshot of the live database from some point in the past. Now such things have to be anonymised.

Chapter 11: PHPMND for Magic Number Detection

PHPMND is a piece of software that comes from the Unix philosophy of "Do one job, well."

It doesn't pretend to be an all-purpose code quality tool but concentrates on one thing - namely the inspection of PHP source code for numbers that aren't in constants.

Assuming that you have your code in the current directory, it runs as follows:

```
phpmnd .
```

… and you'll get a return (hopefully) along the lines of:

```
phpmnd 2.1.0 by Povilas Susinskas
-------------------------------------------
Total of Magic Numbers: 0
Time: 2.02 seconds, Memory: 20.00 MB
```

If, of course, you have software with magic numbers in it, then the output will not only show the count, but list the file and line and show the problematic code:

```
phpmnd 2.1.0 by Povilas Susinskas
------------------------------------------

src/mybadfile.php:28. Magic number: 20
> 28| if ($naughtyvariable == 20) {



------------------------------------------

Total of Magic Numbers: 1
Time: 1.11 seconds, Memory: 20.00 MB
```

In this case, the 28 refers to the line number on which I've put the (obviously problematical) code.

PHPMND tests

PHPMND can check for magic numbers in different places. Some of these are checked for by default, others have to be explicitly included as a command-line option.

The checks can be made:

- In arguments to functions at time of calling
  - round ($price, 2);
- In arrays
  - $myArray = [400,401,402];
- In direct variable assignments
  - $ myPort = 443;
- In default parameters to functions / methods as part of their definition
  - function renderPrice($string, $defaultRounding = 2);
- In general operations (such as multiplying a number by 100)
  - $cm = $inches * 2.54;
- In definitions of properties
  - private $precision = 2;
- * In function returns
  - return 7;
- * In conditionals
  - if ($numberofResults < 10) {...}
- * in switch cases:
  - case 7

The asterisks (*) against the last three indicate that they (and only they) are enabled by default.

It's worth remembering that a number that appears in the middle of a string is not detected as a magic number. So be careful of things set in strings out of which numbers are then parsed.

To run with extra checks enabled, we need to use a command line option like[55]:

```
--
extensions=default_parameter,condition,operati
on,return,argument
```

Unusually among PHP code-checking command line tools, PHPMND returns "success" (ie 0) to the shell running it unless you tell it not to.[56]

```
    phpmnd . --non-zero-exit-on-violation
[options]
```

---

[55] This is what droneforphp gives. See more about this in Part III.

[56] While this is more likely to be an issue in CI environments, it's mentioned here for those who want to automate a bunch of tests via a shell script prior to code checkin.

Chapter 12: PHPMD for various SOLID checks

Any tool that calls itself "PHP Mess Detector" clearly has a strong point of view about what "mess" is.

The point of view is based on the SOLID principles, but with a selection of different (and configurable) "types of mess" the tool can detect.

For our purposes, these break down into four main groups[57], which PHPMD calls.

- Clean code
- Code size
- Unused code
- Design rules

---

[57] There is a fifth, called "Controversial Rules", which I don't recommend. Mostly, this is because they are about the sorts of things that the Coding Standards, and thus tools like PHPCS (see next chapter) handle better.

Some judgement is needed on whether all of the rules (or even all the groups) are appropriate. It's possible to run PHPMD to test for all the groups at the same time, but (particularly when taking on a legacy code base) I find it easier to run four tests independently, and then decide:

- Whether your code must pass all of them.
- What your priority order is for fixing the backlog that's typically created when you run them for the first time.

CleanCode

CleanCode rules contain three non-contentious rules, and one that is a matter of great debate. All four are discussed in Chapter 8 and are:

- Avoiding Static Access
- Avoid else clauses in objects[58]
- Duplicate array keys
- Boolean arguments that change what a function calculates

---

[58] The debated one

So, here's some sample code that deliberately contains something intended to error:

```php
<?php

namespace OurOrg\FrontEnd;

class DemoClassToFailTests
{
    public function justSayNo($flag)
    {
        if ($flag == 1) {
            return "Bobble";
        } else {
            return "Bibble";
        }
    }
}
```

And, as expected, we find:

```
phpmd /project text cleancode
/project/frontend/includes/CommonClasses/
OurOrg/FrontEnd/DemoClassToFailTests.php:
11   The method justSayNo uses an else
expression. Else is never necessary and
you can simplify the code to work without
else.
```

Whether or not you prefer Else expressions in PHP[59] or "single point of return" on functions is for you and your team. If you have no strong preference, it may be better to go with the "tool default."[60]

---

[59] In some languages else expressions are vital. PHP isn't really one of them.

[60] Which feels like the tail wagging the dog, but also feels like "easy to demonstrate you're taking the question of code quality seriously to investors or compliance people."

Code size / complexity

Chapter 7 talked about (coincidentally) 7 different counts of complexity. PHPMD uses all of these, and more (including a composite score called Weighted Method Count.)

For the reasons discussed in Chapter 7, I tend to regard this set of "rules" as useful info for an experienced person to make a decision, not a question of "failing code review" because a parameter is exceeded.

Unused code

Unused code is back to less contentious territory (see Chapter 6.)

PHPMD detects unused "things" in:

- Private fields
- Local variables
- Private methods
- Parameters to methods (including constructors)

In each case, "unused" means that the "thing" is declared, but then never referenced.

It's worth noting that there are some situations in which PHPMD can give false positives.

A good example is where function names are passed, quoted, as parameters to other functions (such as uasort.)

Design rules

The term "design rules" (as used by PHPMD) feels like a blanket term used by the authors of the tool to roll up a large number of unconnected things.

Everything from Goto statements[61] to use of print_r[62] is in here.

The most common issue we actually catch in development is the use of "Assignment in If Statements", which (as noted in Chapter 8), most often mean a missing = sign. For this reason alone, it's worth running the Design Rules set in PHPMD.

---

[61] They're bad, OK. I'm old enough to have started programming in languages where they were the only flow control method. These were not "the good old days."

[62] A very useful debugging technique. It's easier to read blocks in a browser than a terminal log.

Chapter 13: PHPCS for Coding Standards violations

As noted in Chapter 1, there are a range of different coding standards to choose from.

PHPCS (PHP Coding Sniffer) is a tool that will check against many of them defaulting to PEAR. In the examples that follow, I'm going to assume that you are using the PSR-2 standard.[63]

Running PHPCS

Running PHPCS is simple, providing you remember to include the standard(s) against which you are checking as a command-line option.

```
phpcs --standard=PSR1,PSR2 .
```

If it finds errors, it will list them, broken down by files. It's worth noting that, particularly if you are checking against PSR1 and PSR2, then it may effectively duplicate the error messages.

---

[63] While the standard is hyphenated, PHPCS uses the non-hyphenated text PSR2 in its options.

So, in the example below, two of the four errors are simply
that there wasn't a space between the function name and the
opening parenthesis.

```
    FILE:
...es/CommonClasses/OurOrg/FrontEnd/DemoClassToFailTest
s.php
    -------------------------------------------------------
------------------
    FOUND 4 ERRORS AFFECTING 1 LINE
    -------------------------------------------------------
------------------
    7 | ERROR | [ ] Method name
    | | "DemoClassToFailTests::BooleansJustSayNo" is
not in
    | | camel caps format
    7 | ERROR | [ ] Expected "function abc(...)"; found
"function abc
    | | (...)"
    7 | ERROR | [x] Expected 0 spaces before opening
parenthesis; 1
    | | found
    7 | ERROR | [x] Opening brace should be on a new
line
```

PHPCBF - fixing (some of) the style errors automatically

PHPCS is just the analyser, but there's a "sister" tool called
PHPCBF (the CBF stands for "code beautifier and fixer."

It will attempt to fix some of the problems that PHPCS found.

In the PHPCS example above, you may have noticed a column
in the output that was a pair of square brackets, some of
which had a lower-case x between them.

The ones with [x] are the ones that PHPCS believes that PHPCBF should be able to fix.

So PHPCS ends with a set of lines like:

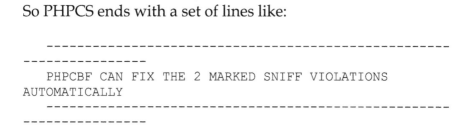

```
    ----------------------------------------------------
----------------
    PHPCBF CAN FIX THE 2 MARKED SNIFF VIOLATIONS
AUTOMATICALLY
    ----------------------------------------------------
----------------
```

There are alternatives to PHPCBF, but they tend to have subtle differences in the default rulesets, so without a lot of custom configuration, you can end up in a situation where PHPCS claims there are errors, and your "fixing software" claims there aren't.

While there are PHPCS errors that PHPCBF can't fix, PHPCS is aware of them and clearly flags them.

Some editors and most IDEs can be set up to autoformat in a particular way and/or invoke PHPCBF automatically.

Chapter 14: PHPCPD for copy/paste detection

Chapter 6 talked about the problems caused by code duplication.

PHPCPD is simply a tool that scans a codebase and attempts to find duplicated blocks.

It's straightforward to run, very fast, and lightweight memory-wise.

```
phpcpd /workspace
phpcpd 2.0.4 by Sebastian Bergmann.
0.00% duplicated lines out of 20070 total
lines of code.
Time: 308 ms, Memory: 19.00MB
```

It has command line options for things like the minimum number of lines that much be identical to trigger a duplicate (which defaults to 5), and the minimum number of tokens (defaulting to 70.)

I've found these defaults sensible.

PART III: Automation

The premise of automation is simple:

- There are things that "the computers our budget allows for" are good at.
- There are things that "the humans in our team" are good at.
- We should automate the routine things that computers are good at.

While the detail changes (computers get faster, team members come and go), the general principle is that it doesn't make sense to pay a human being to do something that can be automated "enough to be useful."

And in the specific case of code quality, that means that we need to look at the value, not just the cost.

The programmers (and thus the CTO and thus the organisation) get value out of seeing the results of tests (because it allows them to identify problems early.)

The high-value item is the test-results.

The automation of test *running* is removing a low-value task and allowing the humans to concentrate on a higher-value one – the interpretation of those results.

The class of software that automates software testing (in all its forms) is called "CI" or "Continuous Integration."

Every single piece of software listed in Part II of this book is software that we run through CI systems.[64]

---

[64] Different clients use different systems. Modern CI systems are basically "open" to allowing this, rather than attempting to embody all the possible types of test.

Chapter 15: Continuous Integration (CI)

One of the frustrations of software development in teams comes when two changes are made, both of which seem to work (with the existing code), but which, when put together, cause some problems.

One key approach is to test on an ongoing basis.

In the days where testing had to be run by hand, getting teams of people together to spend days running through scenarios by hand was an expensive option, used for the final phases of project delivery.

Section II of this book, however, went through a number of tools that have proved useful in the PHP world. Clearly, running a tool to execute a batch of tests is easier, faster and cheaper than running each of those tests by hand.

The next level of automation, though, is to take the responsibility for running the tests away from the manual to-do lists, and onto some form of service.

The type of service that auto-runs these tests is called a CI (Continuous Integration) service.

A common practice is to have programmers work locally, and then push their changes to a git repository. Most CI tools can be configured as hooks from code repositories to automatically fire off tests in response to various events.

In the git world, there are two obvious events that might trigger a CI run:

- A git push (ie - any update to a branch in the repository)
- A git pull (ie - an explicit request to merge code)

On a medium size project (the sort with "a few programmers") a CI system can run all the tools from Part II of this book in under a couple of minutes, even on an Amazon micro instance.

As such, I recommend (and run) a "run on pushes as well as pulls" approach.

Having adopted this policy, we'd expect all the tests to succeed before anyone issues a pull request to merge that branch into master.

There are, outside the scope of this book, other tools that could take several hours to run. If you need to run them, then a less frequent set of runs is probably mandated.

Chapter 16: The main CI tools for PHP projects

There are, of course, many options, and various decisions to be made about requirements.

Firstly, there's the classic hosting hierarchy:

1. Buy hardware, install it into machine room in your office
2. Buy hardware, install it into co-location facility
3. Rent hardware (normally as virtual machines) from a service like AWS, Microsoft Azure or Google Cloud
4. Use a software as a service

Secondly, there is the choice between "free" and "paid" products (or free and paid versions of the same product.) It's worth noting that some tools, particularly those deployed as SaaS ones, charge for usage on open-source projects.

Thirdly, though, we have a key one. Do you want a CI tool that allows different tests to be run on different branches? Some tools have a central configuration of tests, and those tests will be run on all code releases. Others allow a configuration file to be part of the code branch. I prefer this approach, not least because it means that the detailed configuration of the CI suite can live in the same repository as the rest of the code-base, rather than being something that lives out in a configuration file on some infrastructure.

The main tools are:

- Jenkins (which was a fork of Hudson, an Oracle tool.) Jenkins is probably the most popular CI tool, but only runs on your hardware, and maintains a single configuration.
- TravisCI is a hosted service that is free to open-source projects, but chargeable for proprietary ones. It allows branch-specific configuration.
- GitLab CI is a hosted service, but only available as part of GitLab's overall service (which offers a 30-day free trial, but then becomes payable.)
- Drone.io which is available either as a hosted service (free to OpenSource projects), or can be run on your own hardware.

My preferred tool is drone.io, and the rest of this chapter concentrates on that.

Drone.io overview

Drone is a lightweight CI, that runs on Docker.

Drone is, not only a Docker image itself[65], but relies on Docker images to run the individual tests. It relies on a database connection (which will, by default be a SQLLite database that needs to put a couple of files on the host machine.)

---

[65] The installation instructions onto your own hardware are four lines, two of which are "docker pull…" and the other two of which are "docker run." (albeit with a bunch of command-line options.) There's a bit of configuration to get it to talk to your chosen git service. I'm not going to duplicate those instructions here.

Once Drone is installed, it presents a web interface, and initial configuration is done through that interface. The initial configuration is basically about hooking it up to the right Git service.

After that, the CI configuration lives in a single file within the Git repository. This configuration file is called .drone.yml and contains details of the steps that the CI should run when triggered.[66]

A small .drone.yml file for PHP might look like the following:

```
kind: pipeline
name: DroneForPHP
steps:
- name: PSR2
  image:  herloct/phpcs
  commands:
  - phpcs --standard=PSR1,PSR2 /drone/src
- name: Copy paste detection
  image: rvannauker/phpcpd
  commands:
  - phpcpd /drone/src
```

This file has two "steps" it in - one that runs PHPCS (see Chapter 13) to test for PSR2 compliance, and the other which runs PHPCPD (see Chapter 14) to test for code duplication.

One of the issues with using tools such as docker is, of course, the question of which images are appropriate for use.

Alas, the drone team aren't really PHP users, and the official documentation doesn't talk in any detail about tools beyond PHPUNIT.

---

[66] The triggering is done by adding a callback URI to GitHub / GitLab / your chosen git service.

Building a drone configuration for PHP

Because the tools in Part II of this book are maintained as standalone tools, the official support for making them available as Docker images is patchy. In addition, the requirements of a command-line tool intended for eyeballing by a programmer are a little different from the requirements of a CI system (in which one of the most important things is the exit code thrown.)

It's also the case that, as new versions of PHP are released, the tools can work, but give overly verbose notifications, not because of the code being checked, but because of the code in the tool itself.

Keeping your CI config up to date is a low-effort task, but not a zero-effort one.

While I've included a .drone.yml file as Appendix 2, there's a (completely free to use) service that allows you to build your own that was basically written in parallel Part III of this book.

Some things are better delivered as code than delivered as prose.

This tool can be found at droneforphp.com, whose core (at time of writing) looks like:

Select test(s)

- PSR2
- Embedded Configuration
- Clean Code
- Complexity / Size
- Unused Code
- SOLID Design Rules
- Code duplication

Generated drone.yml

```yaml
kind: pipeline
name: DroneForPHP
steps:
- name: PSR2
  image:  herloct/phpcs
  commands:
  - phpcs --standard=PSR1,PSR2 /drone/src
- name: CleanCode
  image: denisura/phpmd
  commands:
# Need to grep out "Unexpected token" errors in newer versions o
# Because the grep exits with error code 0, we have to generate
  - phpmd /drone/src text cleancode | grep -v "Unexpected token"
  - ROWS=`wc -l < /tmp/result`
  - cat /tmp/result
  - if [ $ROWS -gt 1 ] ; then exit 1 ; fi
```

Copy YAML to clipboard

Summary

The reputation of PHP as a "language for amateurs", while not entirely untrue, doesn't need to be true.

There are a good number of programming practices that we can adopt, and get our teams to adopt, to help reduce the long-term cost of maintaining a codebase.

These practices include:

- Considering things off the happy path
- Having a common coding style
- Getting an appropriate mix of testing (which includes, but isn't limited to, unit testing) in place
- Removing embedded configuration and Magic Numbers
- Removing duplicate code
- Removing unused code
- Ensuring that code complexity is manageable
- Using SOLID principles
- Making sure we're connecting to other services in a secure, sustainable way

Actually doing this stuff requires good people...

... but ensuring that this stuff has all been done is, in many cases, a candidate for automation.

Getting the right mix of things done by humans and automated systems is a key skill for CTOs, and the balance is changing with each passing year.

It is generally much easier to install a server / service than it is to change the behaviour of smart people by use of checklists.

So, while it's possible to run many of the tools by hand (and many programmers may choose to do so), having a CI system in place can save a lot of time, and lead to higher quality code.

Appendix 1: Evolving the standards

The IT profession is one of change. What worked in BASIC isn't good for PHP. What works in C++ isn't automatically great for PHP.

But what worked in PHP4 isn't automatically right for PHP7 (even if it executes.) While changing a major version of a programming language in a live product is seldom as pain-free as one might hope, there always comes a point where the security vulnerabilities of an old version of a language make it unsafe for production code. There's also the economic argument that it's harder to find programmers to work in legacy versions of a language.)

PHP has got faster over time, with a significant jump between 5 and 7, so changing major versions can have a good impact on hosting costs.

Changing standards for fashion, however, is just as problematical. Many projects seem to run for the benefit of the CVs of the technology team rather than for the good of the organisation.

But quite apart from languages themselves changing (or frameworks, or database types, or libraries, or architecture...) there's the fact that coding standards (by which I mean more than just coding style) change over time.

Consider code complexity: as the team evolves, there may be a need to simplify code further, or it may become acceptable to relax the requirements a little. For example, you may decide that you can increase the maximum cyclomatic complexity allowed in a class.

So, there needs to be a process for changing the standard.

That process may be as simple as "ask the CTO, who will say yes/no", or may be a matter for architecture review boards and formal workflows...

... but the key idea is that the current standard should be visible and clear, and thus documented. And, of course, the documentation and the configuration of the CI system should match.[67]

---

[67] And don't forget the programmers who have various tools installed locally - they need the same thresholds as the CI system is enforcing centrally.

Appendix 2: What we changed about our own processes as a result of writing this book

Writing a book like this involved doing a lot of thinking about how we[68] were applying the principles and using the tools ourselves.

One of the key learnings surprised us. Namely that we ended up stopping using one of the tools we had been using. We had been using a tool called PHPMetrics to generate a large volume of information about project complexity. We discovered that we were capturing, and logging this information, but never actually using it.

It's a beautiful tool in real-time, but we found it just too seductive, and that we were spending more and more time admiring the analysis, rather than just getting on with the work of coding. That's to say that while things like the average cyclomatic complexity per class were interesting, what was more important was the outliers - picking the classes whose complexity had got out of hand, and focusing on cleaning / re-factoring them until they were more straightforward. We were using PHPMD for this.

---

[68] werarewe.com, a company of which I'm CTO.

However, because it wasn't a "pass/fail" tool but just an information logger, we took the view that it was better to leave it running as part of our CI suite. (It takes about 3-4 seconds to run on each git checkin, and it all happens in the background.) So, if we ever want to look at the metrics it generates, they are there (not only for the current codebase, but for any point in the past.)

We've stopped looking at it as part of our code review sessions.

Appendix 3: A sample (production) .drone.io configuration file

As noted in Chapter 16, I don't recommend you use this file "as is", but instead pick a set of options more useful for you at droneforphp.com

```
kind: pipeline
name: DroneForPHP
steps:
- name: PSR2
  image:  herloct/phpcs
  commands:
  - phpcs --standard=PSR1,PSR2 /drone/src
- name: Embedded Configuration (Magic Numbers)
  image: dockerizedphp/phpmnd
  commands:
  - phpmnd /drone/src --non-zero-exit-on-
violation --
extensions=default_parameter,condition,operati
on,return,argument
- name: CleanCode
  image: denisura/phpmd
  commands:
# Need to grep out "Unexpected token" errors
in newer versions of PHP
```

```
# Because the grep exits with error code 0, we
have to generate the exit code by parsing the
output
  - phpmd /drone/src text cleancode | grep -v
"Unexpected token" > /tmp/result
  - ROWS=`wc -l < /tmp/result`
  - cat /tmp/result
  - if [ $ROWS -gt 1 ] ; then exit 1 ; fi
- name: CodeSize (Complexity)
  image: denisura/phpmd
  commands:
# Need to grep out "Unexpected token" errors
in newer versions of PHP
# Because the grep exits with error code 0, we
have to generate the exit code by parsing the
output
  - phpmd /drone/src text codesize | grep -v
"Unexpected token" > /tmp/result
  - ROWS=`wc -l < /tmp/result`
  - cat /tmp/result
  - if [ $ROWS -gt 1 ] ; then exit 1 ; fi
- name: Unused code
  image: denisura/phpmd
  commands:
# Need to grep out "Unexpected token" errors
in newer versions of PHP
# Because the grep exits with error code 0, we
have to generate the exit code by parsing the
output
  - phpmd /drone/src text unusedcode | grep -v
"Unexpected token" > /tmp/result
  - ROWS=`wc -l < /tmp/result`
  - cat /tmp/result
  - if [ $ROWS -gt 1 ] ; then exit 1 ; fi
- name: SOLID Design Rules
  image: denisura/phpmd
  commands:
# Need to grep out "Unexpected token" errors
in newer versions of PHP
```

```
# Because the grep exits with error code 0, we
have to generate the exit code by parsing the
output
  - phpmd /drone/src text design | grep -v
"Unexpected token" > /tmp/result
  - ROWS=`wc -l < /tmp/result`
  - cat /tmp/result
  - if [ $ROWS -gt 1 ] ; then exit 1 ; fi
- name: Copy paste detection
  image: rvannauker/phpcpd
  commands:
  - phpcpd /drone/src
```

Thanks to...

Any non-trivial project has multiple people involved, and this book is no different.

I've learnt about how to do this stuff by a mix of doing it and asking questions of people who are better at it than me. The most valuable thing in my phone are their contact details.

There are three of them, however, that I particularly want to call out by name.

Mary Harrison, Greg Wright, and Patrick Heesom are all very experienced programmers / engineering managers, who've seen languages rise and fall, but kept their skills current. I was privileged to have all three of them work for me at FundingKnight. I was overjoyed when all three agreed to review this book. The book is much improved as a result of their feedback.

Though, in deference to them, I should point out that none of them agree with 100% of what I'm presenting as "best practice." All three of them gave feedback as a personal favour to me, not because they were paid to proof-read anything, so the errors and strong opinions in the book are mine.

www.ingramcontent.com/pod-product-compliance
Lightning Source LLC
Chambersburg PA
CBHW071141050326
40690CB00008B/1525